The Age of Discovery

...I too, having lost my faith
in language, have placed my faith in language.

– Terrance Hayes

THE AGE OF DISCOVERY

Alan Michael Parker

Tupelo Press

North Adams, Massachusetts

The Age of Discovery
Copyright © 2020 Alan Michael Parker All rights reserved.

Library of Congress Catalog-in-Publication data available upon request.
ISBN-13: 978-1-946482-39-6

Cover painting by Felicia van Bork, "The Voyage 1," 2003
(encaustic on braced panel)
Cover and text design by Bill Kuch

First paperback edition October 2020

Tupelo Press
P.O. Box 1767
North Adams, Massachusetts 01247
(413) 664-9611 / Fax: (413) 664-9711
editor@tupelopress.org / www.tupelopress.org

Tupelo Press is an award-winning independent literary press that publishes
fine fiction, non-fiction, and poetry in books that are a joy to hold
as well as read. Tupelo Press is a registered 501(c)(3) nonprofit
organization, and we rely on public support to carry out our mission
of publishing extraordinary work that may be outside the realm of the large
commercial publishers. Financial donations are welcome
and are tax deductible.

for Felicia, Ti amo

Contents

THE AGE OF DISCOVERY

For Now

Dear Reader,
let me take you in my arms.

Of course,
everybody's suffering.

Wouldn't you like
to stretch out?
To relax?

Dear Reader, I know you're dying.
That's sad. Me too.

How about we wait here together?

When Everyone Wrote a Poem

The drugstore clerk wrote a poem,
every pill a magical hill,

and the librarian wrote a poem
about the one book
kept home,

and the announcer at the dog track
wrote a barking poem
and then another barking poem
chasing the first barking poem,
two circular poems,

and the Supreme Court Justice
wrote a poem to hear our cries,

and the drone operator wrote a poem nearby,

and the pilot wrote a poem called, "Sunrise, Wait for Me,"

and the porcupine wrote a hundred poems,

and the sunflower wrote a brave poem to the lion,

and blue wrote a poem to yellow that ends in green,

and the dollar wrote a poem to a widow,

and all of the poems
lay down
with all of the poems,

and with so many poems,
the moon could finally close her eyes,

and let the world be ours.

We Are Like People Waiting

We are like people waiting for a table,
for the others to finish and slide by,
drawing the strings of their backpacks,
logging on to check the weather,
sweaters and jackets shrugged into,
worn like ghosts, don't forget the umbrella.
We hold the door as they head out,
sneak a peek to see what they ordered
and barely touched. The special today is—
that's all we can read from here.

Inside, family style, we sup with strangers,
share photos, shopping tips,
like cousins who have met at last,
and finish with a saucer of orange slices
so planetary and so biblical and
so tangy. Cash only, counted out:
seventeen, eighteen, nineteen.
And now the next crowd
huddles by the door, and now
it's really raining.

In this way our dreaming
and our waking selves
take turns.

The Microeconomics of Love

I put a poem
in your backup jewelry box,
the one you keep
at the bottom of the taxes from 2003
in order to foil the inevitable burglars,
no one is safe anymore,

and then I found a drawing of a lion
between my two best pairs of underwear,
and, Lord, he was a'roaring,

and so I put a poem in the tall ugly vase
you love for black-eyed Susans,
and then I found a drawing
in the secret zip pocket of my ratty softball bag,
and so I put a poem in your favorite green mitten,
stuffed in the thumb,
and then I found a drawing
in the cheese drawer,
wrapped around the cheddar I like,

and so I put a poem in your Austen,

and then I found a drawing of a wave and a bird
in my sunglasses case,
but I didn't ask why a wave or a bird, I trust you,
and I didn't ask where my sunglasses had gone,

and so I put a poem in your socket wrenches box,
and then I found a drawing in the sugar bowl,
and I'm the only one who takes sugar, one lump,

and so I went to the calendar
to put a reminder

to put a poem
in your grandmother's teacup ten years from now,
but on that day there was already a note
to wrap a drawing around my toothbrush
ten years from now.

What's a man in love to do?
I took down that family photo you never liked,
and I stashed our cellphones in the dead microwave,
and I dumped the Olde Tyme knick-knacks
and all of the mirrors
into a green garbage bag dragged to the curb,

and I threw the television into the neighbor's yard,
and I threw the alarm clock into the other neighbor's yard,
and I tossed the toaster into the first neighbor's yard,
to confuse that neighbor, since no one likes that neighbor,
and I flushed the cheap wine from our former friend,
and I burned the checkbook,

and then I rassled us some vittles,
and then I opened the windows
and I let the air out of every worry.

When I Am a Hummingbird

I love two dogs, even when they're killing
a baby possum near the columbines,
shaking the varmint
until the death squeal chokes to a gargle,

and both dogs stand before the bloody marsupial
nosing it to move,

because that's Nature, right?
(And whom did I just ask whether that was right?)
(And what's a moral quandary for a possum?)

I love the dog who leans,
matter-of-fact in her need,
and the big smile of the small pit bull.

But when I am a hummingbird, finally,
I will beat my wings
eighty times per second,

thousands of seconds
and eighty thousands and thousands

of my splendiferous beating wings,
faster than all of the eighty thousand
beautiful things in the world,

and no one will stop me or catch me
or take my picture, I will be too fast,

and I will dive into the meat
of the possum
and beat there,
the mean, bloody thing alive again.

Birth of the Cool

It must be so hard to be Miles Davis,
and a ghost, and to sit in my kitchen
as I squeal along on a dimestore horn

to one of his greatest tracks, "Venus de Milo" (1957),
on a rainy Saturday in Obscurity, U.S.A.,
percussed by a high metal trickle in the downspout

and the orgasmic sighs of the coffeepot,
in the too-bright interior light.
(I've gotta, gotta, gotta get a dimmer.)

The dogs snooze on the sofa like session drummers.
Like hipsters, the houseplants wait for whatever.
Miles and I only jammed in my dreams,

but once, on a stoned sojourn to see the Pacific
in a borrowed Saab in 1983
with an aspiring physicist named Maureen,

Birth of the Cool changed who I would be.
(Maureen, where have you gone in like forever?)
Even in my dreams, Miles never turns around

(the music, man, the music),
and I understand, my back to everyone—
but a different life alone, this one, mine.

Now we're listening to *Sketches of Spain:*
time hits shuffle,
and Bella the dog yips with a skip in her sleep

as Miles gets it right again, how the sliding
drops on the windowpane
in me feel.

The Stars

When God's Inbox was empty,
God felt better,
her Big List done for the day,

as the mist spread upon the time zones
and the starlings streamed
back into her chest.

In her pocket, a locket.
In her car, the far sound
of tomorrow, a bell.

Maybe REPLY ALL had been a mistake,
God said to the weather,
who never listens.

She tore herself a chunk of bread,
a hunk of Asiago,
snatched a stem of seedless grapes,

and stepped out upon the back deck
to read, and wait for her deer,
as the buses like caterpillars

chewed home for the night.
God knew the difference
between taking and making:

the sky was hers.
Soon she would unmoor her mind
and bob and drift among the stars,

to where
she could only imagine,
free of herself.

Independent Survey

Press **3** now. Press *** 9** now.

At any time in this survey, press **4**.

If you want a really good sandwich, press **7**. Press **2** for tuna.

If you were to have dinner with anyone, why not with me?

If you were a different person and I were a different person, who would have been my mom?

Can you feel love without your body?

To picture yourself having a cool cocktail with a new friend, press **3, 1**.

If stanza eight of every scripture were the secret answer, why didn't the Buddha say so? Press **6** and then press the # sign for *Maybe he did*.

Press **9** for a prize.

If longing is enough, press **2, 2, 3** for *I'm over here*. Press **2** again, and then press **4**.

Keep pressing **7**.

Press **8, 2, 8, 5, 6, 3, 9, 9, 6** for *I remember you, I would love to reconnect, what have you been doing?*

To access your childhood now, press **3, 1**.

To eliminate every single invisible negativity wave in the galaxy, press **3, 1**.

To return to the present, press **3, 1**.

Press **3, 1** to sign up for consciousness beyond technology.

Press **4** to do this all again.

Poem

1. Dad, Don't Be That Guy
2. Dad, Quoting the Wikipedia Isn't Gospel
3. Dad, I'm Going to Take Those Away
4. Dad, I Warned You
5. Dad, the Doctor Said
6. I Couldn't See This Coming, Not So Soon
7. When Do I?
8. Dad, There's Life, and There's Also Poetry
9. Sponge Bath
10. Hello, I Can't Find My Pills
11. I Signed That Form
12. You Know You Didn't Sign That Form
13. Sign the Form
14. She Never Learned Where the Dishes Go
15. If You Can't Do This, the Doctor Says
16. I Left It Next to Your Bed
17. I Promise, Dad
18. Dad, Where's Your Hat?
19. Dad, Did You Leave Your Hat in the Waiting Room?
20. No, This Is Not the Waiting Room

Or

The movie's boring and her date's boring
and she doesn't like snacking
but needs something;

on line for refreshments she looks around
and there is a woman who could be her mom,
her dead mother, gone four years July.
Luckily, there are decisions:
popcorn, lemonade.
The credit card machine beeps
and she takes two long breaths
and turns to her dead mother and says, "You look–"

but the other woman holds up a hand, stop.
"I know," says the other woman. "Right?"
"You look exactly like my mother,"
says the other woman.
"She died when I was twelve."

Each, in the other's eyes, a dead mother
blinking in the candy-colored light.
"I wish—" the first woman says,
but doesn't know what to wish.
Then she remembers: "I've seen you
before, at the airport bar in Atlanta."
The other woman nods, yes:
"I travel a lot. It's possible."

The Trees of Kraków

I was naked in bed, where I panic less,
reading, and wanting to go somewhere fun
next summer, because fun will help us age.

Let us go to Kraków together,
since I know a squidge of Polish,
I know the word "cupcake" in Polish is *babeczka*—

babeczka, I say to the prettier of my big toes.
In Kraków, I read, "The City Council has proposed
a 'renewal' of the trees surrounding the Błonia

by removing all of them at once."
What will become of the sparrows of Kraków?
The sparrows stumble about the Błonia

as the trenchcoated accountants of Kraków
pedal furiously to the mortuary, elbows wide.
The alphabetical schoolgirls of Kraków

line up to visit the next monument,
and the Vistula River agrees with itself again.
The traffic cops of Kraków wave on, wave on.

Love, lie next to me, I am sorry I am so
cuckoo with the clock. Let us plan a trip
to Kraków, before democracy kills us all.

Love, in the oven
of my chest, I have baked
a cupcake, *babeczka*, take a bite.

What Good is Life without Painting

I was participating fully in Life,
or so my calendar said,

when I had the spiritually extravagant
gift of being heartstruck,
standing before a painting.
Wow, everything I could see was different.
Now that's art! I declared too loudly,

and the people on the patio heard me,
they were rearranged too,
chitchatting with Manhattans and old ideas,
they decided not to sell off the planet,

and the people in the time share
were preternaturally glad to be a social organism,
as they rushed to their windows
and then to their email,
and they agreed upon an expedition
to a secret waterfall
(turkey on rye, swimming, awe),

and the people in the break room—
well, to be fair, only Mrs. Saunders,
who has had such a time—
decided to go to night school for social work.

The painting I was watching
was all green and all brown and all blue
at once. Feelings
happened there, and in me.
It was like being a plum, and ripening.

I Just Got Here

I am like a man who has pulled off the road,

nosed his car into the bushes
and left the engine running,
in such a hurry

that he stumbled and skittered down the hill,
tripping once on some damn roots,
landing hard, jamming his left wrist,

but making his way through the birches
to kneel at the creek and cup his hands,
splashing water on his face,

to lie on the spongy moss
just for a little while,
and try not to fall asleep,

because who knows
what's on the other side of sleep.
But it's too hard not to fall asleep:

rubbing his eyes with his fingertips.
to stay awake

when all of the talking and the listening
and the not listening
make him so tired.

The car's still running: he knows that.
His life's up there, in that car,
and he'll go back, and he'll drive on

in a minute, just one minute more.

Against Ekphrasis

Outside, a bluebird and an indigo bunting
take turns at the feeder, confusing me,
which one is blue. I blame the sky,

I do, every time I try
to marry the sky to a particular blue,
it's gone, and then me too.

When I was a boy poet
in a canoe, and the blue stars
were oh-so in the river,

and the river was oh-so to the sea,
my open mouth went O to every blue.
I made the blue woohoo.

But now, because of the birds
looping through the gazebo
and out, anew,

I know I was wrong.
Because blue is a unit of time.
Because each blue measures

how long is blue,
flashing outside my window,
pretending to be a bird.

The Set-up

A poet, a goose, and a toaster walk into a bar.
A baseball and an iguana share a park bench.
A politician and a bee trade lives.

A woman with a cup of fear tries not to spill.
A man with an empty pocket doesn't come home.
A poet and his shadow walk into a bar.

A rabbi and a martini row out to sea.
A mouthwash says to a penguin, hey.
A politician and a fire truck trade jobs.

An English Springer Spaniel barks at a lemon.
An abacus says to a shotgun, hey.
A poet and a refugee walk into a bar.

An uncle steals a fern from the office.
A lamp and a Meerschaum pipe abandon a painting.
A politician and a refugee trade lives.

A cough says to an E.R. doctor, hey.
A sex worker says to a river, sure.
A poet, a refugee, and a cup of fear.
A politician with a shotgun walks into a bar.

Top Hat and Tails

It's the moment in a rented tux
when you catch sight of your vanity
in the beat-up Chevy's side-view mirror,

adjust the pleats of the yellow cummerbund,
arms stiff in a smart shirt,
and lock the car with the chunky clicker,

then, chin down, turn yourself and aim
for the scrum of the evening gowns,

only to find it's a softball game,
lit up and easy
in the juicy evening, in the made-up light,

and the field is the biggest bowl of candy ever,
and Mark is there, and Big Weasel, and Doctor Jim.

It's a softball game, you're on deck,
your team's losing,
but you're so fine in a tux—

that's what the wrong word
in a poem is like.

Maybe the Soul

Four miles more, it's too hard—
on a bike on the Blue Ridge Parkway,
the road ribboning away—

when she thinks suddenly
maybe the soul
is like a handmade scarf,

which makes her stop for a long pull of water,
leaning one-legged
on the gravel shoulder.

If she were a scarf,
reincarnated as a scarf,
she could be a gift someone would love,

a scarf with matching mittens—
but who can believe
in reincarnation.

Or maybe the soul is
one of the colors she sees.
But which one?

Back to the peloton, trying to keep up:
maybe the soul wraps around us,
she thinks, a thought in Nature,

how loose life is.

Family Music

In the dream I have of my mother,
I take her hand in both of mine,
but hers isn't actually a hand.

We're long-lost chums in a recording studio
where the drum kit's ruined,
the snares and bass a heap of cans.

I want to bang on something.
In her eyes, a sunrise,
time to go, and so

I ask my dead mother,
To find you, what should I sing?
Even in death, she won't say.

The Ride

1.

The light's falling off the continent
in L.A., all of the traffic
snarling at the end of the chain,

and the sad, golden glow
of the boarded-up video store

sings like the soul of John Keats,
and like the soul of John Keats

the boarded-up video store
makes sadness look pretty
as we bump by in slow time.

I've been thinking this thought so long:
driving is the new reading.
Here in L.A. tonight, my driver
is my guide, a girl who talks and talks

as though a meter were running,
as though to fill a cup.

Not hurrying home to her mother—
she's on a colostomy bag, now that they know—

a girl whose words need a listener.

2.

Progress is a moment between wars.

My Lyft driver commuted to college

to learn to do windows,
dressing the mannequins.
Is that what words do,
dressing the mannequin?
I feel a pinch,
a life too small.

3.

The drowsy numbness of John Keats
pains my sense, sifts upon L.A.,
floury, neither being nor becoming.
My Lyft driver chats the whole long way

to the after-party
that is the 21st century,

Mom at home
in the doorway of her death,
shielding her eyes, nearly a salute,

as the desert lights up,
metal and glass, all embers,

and the signals urge us apart, and on.

The Trains All Arrived

When the trains all arrived, like giant feelings on every track, the station
master had to rub his glasses clean, surprised, what was happening, worrying a
plaid handkerchief.

At every platform, on all the sidings, in rows, in furrows, gleaming in soot, all
the trains.

Was the light like metal too? It was.

As though the trains had come to burrow in the city, to excavate the alleys,
to root in the lobbies. The trains the keepers of secrets, their patient wheels
thinking.

The station master pulling the string of a window shade, close that, a bad idea.
The brazen pigeons refusing to roust.

What did it mean, that the trains all arrived? What next?

Prudent, the young mother lifted her lolling infant from the stroller, one foot
kicking.

As though our memories all arrived. As though our journeys had not been. As
though we had returned from the border we dream.

Oh, the credulous gaze of the station master.

Did the great vault of the concourse seem tremulous in the tumult, in the oily
stink? It did.

Surely the doors would slide wide and we would board, handing up our cares.
Then the trains would trundle away: our next lives were waiting.

We, who always said we would be going. Yes, we will send for you.

The Future of Love

"Soon we'll be sending everything by email, even love."

— The Rev. Christopher Marks

Dear friend, attached you will find

a wild, blue cloud
and a whiff of local wind that stirs and spins,
and I am sending too
the rutted far field I walked this morning,

counting eleven different yellows on parade,
before the afternoon set to gray.

*

Dear friend, attached:

a box of a local wine,
a round of cheese rolled in ash,
and a small machine
(delighted upon in a general store)
that clicks and hums when done,
whatever it does.

I cannot recommend the wine.

*

Dear friend, attached
I wished to send the impression
the pillow minds
in the gutter a dream furrows.

Challenges arose:
sending a thing in the negative.

I'll try again tomorrow.

*

Dear friend, attached
you will find a window
smeared by childhood.
The locks unlock to the right.

*

Dear friend, attached
you will find the sense of waking,
the room in shadow,

where the bureau and the dresser and the table
share their heavy, deep beliefs.

*

Dear friend, attached
I am sending one whole evening,
itemized. See #17.

*

Dear friend, attached
you will find a wax envelope of leaves
the waning fall cherished:
yellow, singed, and tumbled.

*

Dear Readiness, dear Maybe,
the season is brisk in me.

*

Dear friend, attached
you will find a draught of vintage.
I love the thought of you
holding the past up to the light.

*

Dear friend, attached
you will find so many clouds
I could not believe them all.

Write to me, and let me know
what to think of a sky so full.
It brims as I do,

sending you everything.

Half the World is Ours

Why all the secrets
sewn into the lawns
and into the fields and into the clouds
with needles of light?

Through the cloth, into the air,
through the cloth.
And yes, only part of the world
is knowable, most of the philosophers

agree. But if one god
were to come—not the one
with the sword, but the kind god
offering warm socks, lentil soup,

a chunk of bread and butter,
the one who knows us—
I would ask, *What's for dessert?*
Maybe it's raining, but surely it will.

Maybe there are no gods,
or maybe there is no maybe.
An afternoon is made of waiting
for the other half of the day:

at the corner, a bus shudders,
taking on passengers: there's Dana,
the shy clerk from the pharmacy,
with whom I shared a photo of my son,

and on her phone, her twins,
toothless, glorious ballerinas,
one of them unhappy.
I was buying AA batteries,

a deodorant without aluminum.
Maybe we'll be okay:
that's how our lives are.
The bus pulls away, like everything.

Curses

May you run out of milk.
May the milk you need
be the milk of your shame.
May you zip to the store,
and may the store be out of milk

as you step outside into a wet fog,
not knowing what to do.
There in your life
may there be a cow
shaking her bell at you.

May her bell be the bell of your failure.
May the cow be the cow of your guilt
in the supermarket parking lot.
And do you know what's real?
You do not.
May you not know.

May you run out of milk.
May you fall asleep and forget
and wake to a cow
knocking about your bedroom,
a cow in the shadows,
maybe all shadow,

shaking her bell at you,
until you apologize

to me
for what you said this morning.

Happy

She wants to be unhappy, so she is,
which makes her happy,
and she makes the people around her unhappy,
which makes her happy,
but now she's so happy
she's unhappy,
which isn't the same unhappiness she wants, it's too easy.
She would blame her father for leaving,
but he wouldn't.
She would blame her mother
for loving too hard,
or for never admitting her own unhappiness,
but her mother was clearly unhappy,
and taught her daughter well.
Lots of people are unhappy:
all of the politicians
who can't keep everything they have,
and the priests dreaming of somewhere else,
and the people whose jobs it is
to fix things—cars, or teeth, or diseases—
those people want everyone to be unhappy,
to have things that need fixing,
so that they can fix them and be happy,
those people always wishing everyone unhappiness.
The people who step too close to her
at the store, now they're unhappy,
and letting them do that, letting them
make her unhappy like that,
cutting in front of her,
makes her happy,
which would probably make them unhappy,
if they knew. The people on the news
are unhappy, shouting at each other,
they hate each other,

but what do they know
about unhappiness, she would show them
how to find it, how to
share it, how to make themselves
happy, the labor that is
unhappiness, the joy.

Two Men Disagree, and Row Out to Sea

The boat was right for their anger.
The waves were always and true.
The fish swam in lives no one knew.
Whose turn was it to row?

The boat was a knife or a hammer.
The far and the near didn't matter.
The fish turned together away.
Who in a circle has the last say?

The boat was too small for their anger.
The weather and sea were one.
The waves in the waves would be done.
Whose turn was it to row?

Anger rowed the men.
The sea was the anger to come.
A life is a spoon in a bowl.
Who in a circle has the last say?

The sea is a mouth and an ear.
The sea is the sound without air.
Who in a circle has the last say?
Whose turn is it to row?

Neruda on Capri

1.

It is not age, or wisdom, or marriage
that rings in me, but I am rung.
I have been reading again, instead

of living, following Neruda
in 1952 to Isola di Capri,
in the great boom of the startling sun.

Neruda in exile, suffering from nothing,
his communism too populist
for the tsars of Chile,

sharing a pornographic story with his lover,
Urrutia, in a grove of Taranto myrtle,
and being answered by an unseen bird,

and laughing at himself to be alive.
As though the man himself were an Ode.
Neruda the bell, and I am rung.

2.

I came upon a bee inside
a work glove in my shed:
the sound was small and everywhere.

My reading for the morning had been Shumawicz,
the Soviet exile and survivor of Stalin's gaze
who was rumored to have loved Akhmatova,

and who writes of capitalism,
"A perfect system—designed to guarantee our losses."
The bee was furious. There was a universal

rage inside the glove,
a rising refusal, the insistence
death teaches us.

No god, I let the bee go
to die later, in the summer's long infirmary.
Shumawicz, who was Neruda's drinking partner

on Capri, the limoncello viscous as the night,
also writes, "An economic theory
only matters as a rationale for past crimes."

Cantankerous and warty, Shumawicz believed
he had outlived history, and so, on Mondays
he would set fire to his money.

3.

Matilde Urrutia is singing
the Wedding March from *Lohengrin*,
Jewel of youth, remain here...

and Pablo hums badly along.
Matilde is singing, and they are taking the air
past the ever-present, unhappy carabinieri,

then up the volcanic hill,
the Mediterranean evening a geometric fire
upon the great shade pines,

and then Matilde is singing a Chilean folk song
Pablo cannot abide,
a ditty of a little kitty who saves

a family of mice from an ax.
The song rhymes *camarada* with *palabra,*
comrade with *word,* a rhyme he'll later steal.

Matilde is singing, and the song belongs
to Pablo's first wife, a memory of Purgatory,
duty abandoned, and guilt,

and Pablo drops Matilde's hand.
It is as though the sea has let go
the island.

In her memoir, Matilde writes,
"Even if we were far apart,
our thoughts seemed linked."

4.

Hope is the soul's processional.
Hope is a parade
of possible selves

inside the physical world.
I see hope:
the pollen becoming honey,

or the tide delivering,
the laying out of the future
like a dress upon the sea.

5.

But history—history is sand.
Shumawicz is nothing to us.
By 1952, his pleurisy had taken him

to the island.
In his chest, his elegy.
He and Neruda, famously, would lose

their keys, and the Capri hoteliers
would leave open a room
for the drunken friends.

I think that death might be a room
left open—did Shumawicz?
A thought is sand.

6.

All along, I have been writing about intimacy
but not naming how it terrifies me.
I make up objects, lives,

confections of euphonia,
these jiffs of wit,
nooks for me to hide inside.

7.

Not to Pablo but to Matilde
I return, Matilde in her yellow
dressing gown in the garden,

her tea gone cold, humming,
and scratching their puppy, Nyon,
a dog granted a visa to travel

by the Chilean consul to Rome,
the nation's other greatest poet,
Gabriela Mistral, a.k.a. *Lucila Godoy.*

Matilde the person, not the story.
No one knows where Shumawicz has gone,
but Neruda roars in the bedroom

historically, snoring off his brilliance.

They're connected: she feels
herself rattle in his dream.

Matilde, who was pregnant and
who would miscarry three times,
lived for years in the "vertical house"

Pablo built for her in the Chile she hated,
never happy to go up the stairs,
rueful, writing in her memoir,

"We only cared about the aesthetics."
Matilde, the poet's muse, who learned to believe,
"What a great inconvenience a child would have been."

8.

I am funny: I say to friends,
"I have no friends,
only material."

Neruda on Capri,
the bees in a hive behind
his borrowed house and bed,

each an Ode.
The bee in a poem, put there by me.
The man in the poem,

not the story but the man, Neruda, taken.
I take, and take, and want to own nothing:
Matilde Urrutia, be happy.

A Fable for the Lost

Here's a story about a monk and a cat.
Here's a story about a tree that hopes.
Here's a story about a girl on a roof.

Here's a story about the wind just waiting.
Here's a camera taking pictures of the soul.
Here's a story about a cat and lightning.

In another story the ogre gives away his gold.
In a different story boys hunt for a stag.
Here's a story about a girl on a roof.

In a new story the rain refuses.
Here's an iridescent glimpse of a possible future.
Here's a story about a monk in a hat.

Here's a story about a girl who won't come down.
Here's a story about a girl who won't be told.
Here's a story about a girl who wants to be tall.

Toward the end of the story there's the smell of peppermint.
Here's what the soul feels like to touch.
The monk in the story has no cat.

Here's a story about a roof that sighs.
Here's a story about the rain and endings.
Here's a story about a girl and a cat.
Here's a story about a girl who climbs.

The Names

What name do you call yourself

when you drop a glass and it shatters,
or you lock yourself out, the car still running,

or you drunk-text a former lover?
Mine is "asshole": that's my secret, angry name.

Some of the women I ask
begin their names
with "you"—you this, you that—
and some of the men use their own last names.

Some of my students only claim to bellow, inchoate,
but I suspect that's not true,
or it will change.

I tell you this because

when I am waiting for the train at the end of days,
my ticket and papers lost,
I will have to confess my name to the clerk,
and I fear I will only recall my anger.

Will you remember this conversation?
Will you come see me off?

Ornithology

When a bird flew into my window
and made a hard and soft death sound,

I found her in the dirt below
and I fixed a cardboard nest for her
and fed her from an eyedropper
what the Internet suggested,
and I named her Young Self,

and when a bird flew into my living room
and frantically bumped at every corner above,
I named her Old Self,

and because height and light are
humankind's spiritual aspiration,
I wished my hands were birds.

Luckily, it was evening,
the outside version of my sorrow:

the swallows flocked and flew
to sleep somewhere, presumably,
and every swallow was like a minute,

so I watched and tried to count, which is what I do,
despite so much of each day
happening to me,

and I fed my Young Self more sugar water
while my Old Self
beat in a corner to get out.

Aubade, with Two Deer

Soon I'll need assurances, a shower, coffee, pills.
In the fuzz of dawn, I'm a bell
and time's the clapper, rung until
one state of being over-rings another—

so soon, so soon. Now, and now.
But in the kitchen there are only shadows
out a window, shapes and silhouettes:
mist, some trees, two deer.

How each animal can seem a question,
and that means me.
I'm thinking that the dream has left them, too,
the jittery dream, and in a moment,

they will blur again to woods,
which I would like to do.
Hold still, the whole scene says,
before the sun drives in the first nail.

Nature Hates Me

I am not a large man, as men go,
aside from my ego and my greed,
and my vanity, and my opinions.
It's true that I think my stuff

is better than yours, which is why
you should give me money,
so that I will have the best stuff,
a good result for all.

But how does the deer know
who I am, or the rabbit, or the clouds,
or the minnows in two inches of water,
or time? Nature flees from me:

the weather is always leaving,
the sunlight thinning, threadbare, a ruse.
Just a flick of an ear, and the doe
gambols through the dew, surviving,

because she knows
the murderer I could be,
in my indifference, making stuff up,
imagining she's pure and lovely.

Later, Love

Who among us just had sex?
How about that couple at the picnic table,
with their take-out box

of kimchi rice, sharing a pile of napkins,
or the office temp crying on the L,
the shuddering train her heart,

or all of the stars in the sky
with all of the stars in the sky?
And you two, in the back row, definitely.

There are so many cars—
even the cars
nuzzle in parking lots,

trying not to let us see.
Oh, and never forget the paintings:
the paintings look at one another

across the gallery, and everybody knows.
And the people who see the paintings,
they look at one another too.

Which is all to say this afternoon
I love you after,
when your skin's a rosy smear

of apricot and orange peel,
and I discover
a long hair of yours

in a swoop
upon a page I'm trying to read.
I close the book:

the pages lie together
like the sea and the shore at night
when we're not there.

Things and Feelings

In the ever-leaving of a dream,
I swim across the soft grass,
the water green, my arms my oars,

until the morning light divides me
into here and gone.
Sure, it's ridiculous to wonder,

which may be why I do—
what if the things
we dream of care?

What if the left foot minds the right?
Does the shirt want to be clean?
Think of the comma, overrun,

and the leaves, and the slo-mo ways
they die. The music passes through
and by, the adagio no matter,

and the red blush of the Anjou pear
browns easily in the bowl.
That's it: memory is a bowl.

And feelings are in the bowl.
And the self
evaporates from the surface of a bowl.

Breakfast

It's not just sentimental, no, no, no...

Once there was a blueberry
in a bowl of granola.
The bowl was Melamine, the table was pine,
the kitchen was linoleum and metal and oak,
and the house was brick and cedar and aluminum,
and the roofing material in the shingles
was fire-rated Class A, don't worry.
There were trees: hawthorns and one river birch.
There were azaleas and a Lindley's Butterfly Bush.
The sky was 78% nitrogen and 21% oxygen,
with a trace of argon gas, and ice in crystals.
Space was an almost perfect vacuum,
with a few hydrogen atoms per cubic meter.

Maybe the blueberry and one hydrogen atom
were cousins, cosmically and/or metaphysically.
The spoon that held up the blueberry
was aluminum, the shine a little worn,
and the blueberry was violet in a gradient,
a tad puckered, still with a bit of stem.

Today, class, let's all be astronauts.
We'll begin with breakfast, and then
we'll search the universe for tenderness,
which I suspect—so long,
my blueberry, *adieu*—
may be the last perfect thing.

In the Next Life, a Tree

So I shall put on my tree hat
and my tree shirt and tree pants
and my root boots
and let my gouges show

and walk until I stay
and keep for the birds a home

and every so often
every so
I shall turn a little
to the light to grow

and I shall wrap
I wrap up in wind
so I can listen
to each inclination

blind in the snow
I shall let my colors decide

the years I will wear
all of my rings

and so many arms shall I have
and never need more
to carry
to carry the sky

A Partial Eclipse of the Self

I was feeling all Neo-Platonic on a Friday afternoon,
driving Highway 304 from my job to my fun
with the other prisoners,
bumper to bumper in our anxieties,

and I was trying to sing along to a song I couldn't hear
but all I could muster was an imitation of Nature,
just like a road imitates a river.

What a week. God
had been chasing me all week.
Or not. Because I can't tell, my Captain,
if I chase God or God chaseth me.
Who would know, running so.
Thank you, caller.

This happened idling by the yard sale I call memory.
This happened after the rehearsal I call friendship.
This happened near the rodeo I call success.
This happened by the airport I call history.

And then I remembered I forgot,
and so I called to cancel,
but no one answered.

Drivers of the world,
eyes closed through the roundabout,
filled to the brim
with danger, pull off:

park in the park where you are;
breathe, and stay.

This happened near the bus stop I call teaching.
This happened near the drive-in I call art.
This happened at the intersection I call fatherhood.

This happened driving through a moment, and I want it back.

Virtual Villanelle

Email is the conscience of the race.
I love you more with every update.
Delete, delete. Delete, delete, delete.

Now that we've never met, I think of you
Every time my laptop goes to sleep.
Email is the conscience of the race.

Thank you for the puppies and the .gif.
I hope it's okay I found another site.
Delete, delete. Option-Shift-Left Arrow.

Thank you for the pictures at the zoo:
You are so real. You are so true.
Email is the conscience of the race.

Maybe I could make a meme of us;
Maybe we could monetize our lust.
Delete, delete. Ctrl-Alt-Delete.

I posted my selfie on the internet:
I love you more with every hit.
Email is the conscience of the race.
Delete, delete, delete, delete, delete.

Egypt, North Carolina

Let us pray
for the animals in the kitchen,
that they live another year.
For the wild, unhappy refrigerator,
ice an unsolicited opinion.
For the beatific oven.
For the sulky teen toaster,
full of surprises, never on time.
For the sultry coffeepot, my favorite,
with its secret dream of sex.
For the window with its politics,
us and them.

Soon, it will be my time.
I'll take out the trash,
ill-fated as any Pharaoh,
and stand myself in the can.

The New World

In the diner before work, a hymn is hummed to time,
to the circadian, to shine, to electricity,
to someone else's initials gouged into the pine,

to the usual in the usual booth.
Among head honchos striped for power;
among teens elbowing through puberty,

high on a new license;
among public servants laughing in safety orange,
none of their hopes a task.

The TV knows that someone here
will meet with violence—
look around and pick—

but the TV doesn't say
who will cross herself with surprise,
or whom a stroke will return to monosyllables,

the mortar gone, each word a brick.
The numbers on the TV are the data
are the news, a teeming in our cells,

bottomless as the coffee.
At least we're glowing—
in the amber of the syrup,

in the worn sheen of the linoleum,
giddy as the wake-up song that begins the day,
the second verse slapped away.

A diner is an ark that never sails,

until in twos we stagger to the parking lot,
buttoning up, zipping tight,

chucking a chin to that guy in IT
whose name just might be Ron,
who might have a gun.

The Age of Discovery

Someone will call
and I'll answer,
or I'll call someone,

and Sandy, the neighbor, will go check,
and someone will pull over and wait, an inkling,

and someone opening a box will sneak a Danish,
a little icing on her cheek, right there,

and someone at the deli
will tape a big order above the register,

and someone will speak more softly in a hallway
and walk more slowly when listening,

and someone late for work
will use her teeth on the lid of a coffee,

to peel it back and snap it to,
even the steam thin,

and someone at the clinic
will wash his hands in a shiny sink,

and someone, after,
will stand up and stretch
for what feels like all year,

and step through a window
that wasn't there before.

When the Moon was a Boy

In the morning at the farmers market,
the pears shone on the canted table,
an image from the same dream
the moon kept having and couldn't explain.

He only had a nickel,
enough for two pears,

and he wanted to give the sun a pear,
and he wanted to give the wind a pear,
and he wanted to give the rain a pear,
and the ocean needed a pear.

So the moon climbed the roof of the world
to hide, he was only a boy,
and when he couldn't decide, he ate both pears.

There's so much need, said the boy,
looking down on us,
pear juice dripping from his chin forever.

Old Sink in the Grass, This Morning

Because if I had four legs
and carried nothing

because if my ways
poured through me away

and if a bird sang for comfort
in the mouth of me
in the lion's full yawn

and if my walls were a drum
and I could boom big

if only the elements only

I would keep no wrong
and live my death irrelevant

and then a child again
I would climb in

to fly and salute and bang and ride
in a fire truck on the ocean in time
on a whip of air

if my arms an open barrel
if my arms a sky

in the infinite mind
I would return
I would belong

I Want to Believe That the More Beauty I Encounter, the Better Person I Become

And so I believe.
And I go to museums,
where I feel differently alive.
Look, that's beautiful—

someone made that.
I feel better.
It's a little like dreaming.

But there's ugliness, too,
and I'm in the ugliness,
and it changes me.
The horrible happenings wake me

in the unconsciousness that is a living life,
this sort of sleeping life
I was apparently enjoying,

metaphorical me in my Victorian shirt-dress
and pom-pommed sleep hat
and curly-toed wonder shoes.

In the museum, it's worth asking:
if prolonged exposure to beauty
makes a person better,
what if we dragged the dictator to the sunrise?

But if it's ugliness we need
to know the ugliness, to choose,
maybe there's still hope—

being poked into
at dawn by the shiny fingers of God,
or whatever that is.

What I want is to feel
all of the color-feelings in the sky,
which is a museum of color-feelings,

the long swirly pokes of the god-like stuff
sticking into me,
so beautiful, helping me do good,
now that I've dreamed.

Snow Day

And in the morning the cars were still parked,

and the people stumbling from last night
had nowhere to hide, and so they didn't,

and the airplanes on the runways
pretended to be children, ready to fly,

and a secret smiled in an email,
and the money rubbed together, keeping warm,

and a diamond in a velvet bed
dreamed a geologic dream,

and the mall was a museum,
and nothing else happened for a while,

and the plow came around again and waved,
and the pizza man had no more pizza,

and knowledge knew its feelings,
and the hard drive forgot to hum,

and the little hammer waited next to the heart,
and luck, with a bow, closed the door,

and the light unpinned your hair,
and the light opened my hope,

and your tongue was a key,
and my tongue was a key,

and we were unlocked, and there we stayed.

Psalm

If there are grave stones, may there be
shy stones, kind stones, mad stones,
scared stones, thoughtful stones,
and may we have a choice;

and if there are hummingbirds, may there be
humming walks and humming naps,
humming minutes between
the minutes that hum in anger,
a humming table and chair by the fire,
and a warm and humming towel to wrap us in.

If there are thunder clouds, may there be
whisper clouds and echo clouds,
clouds the rustling of linens,
giggling clouds scampering,
and clouds to call a child home;

if there are heavy sighs, may there be
sighs that float or sink or rise,
and sighs that drift away,
and sighs to take from us our sighs;

and may the weeping willow,
the weeping redbud,
and the weeping cherry
weave of their weeping an evening gown;

and when we come to the end of days,
may we come to a beginning;
and if there is a time keeper,
may there be a time giver,
and if there is a guard house,
may the house be safe unguarded,

and if there is an ocean view, may we see
what the ocean sees,
the little boats of our bodies
nudged into the tide.

Notes

The epigraph comes from Terrance Hayes's "Snow for Wallace Stevens" *Lighthead* (NY: Penguin Books, 2010).

"For Now" is after Eugenie Caraline's "Pietà (With Borzois)," a relatively obscure work in her oeuvre. Caraline, b. 1831-d.1863, is known mostly for her landscapes, many of which contain talismanic symbols yet to be deciphered.

"Birth of the Cool" takes its title from the classic Miles Davis 1957 album, on which "Venus de Milo" appears. *Sketches of Spain*, released in July of 1960, presents Davis's collaboration with the composer Gil Evans. The borrowed Saab in the poem was my sister's.

"Independent Survey" is for Frannie Finnegan.

"The Trees of Kraków" quotes "Saving Kraków's Trees," by a staff writer for *The Kraków Post*. http://www.krakowpost.com/1564/2009/09/saving-krakows-trees.

"What Good is Life without Painting" owes its title to the first line of James Tate's poem, "Read the Great Poets," which begins, "What good is life without music..." *Selected Poems* (Wesleyan: Wesleyan University Press, 1991).

"Against Ekphrasis" is for Sandra Beasley.

"Top Hat and Tails" borrows its title from the great composer Irving Berlin's song, "Top Hat, White Tie and Tails," performed by Fred Astaire in the 1935 film, *Top Hat*. Irving Berlin could neither read nor write music.

"Family Music" is for the late Marjorie Eiseman.

"The Ride" contains a quotation from the opening lines of John Keats's "Ode to a Nightingale": "My heart aches, and a drowsy numbness/Pains my sense..." *The Complete Poems of John Keats* (NY: Penguin Classic, 1977).

"The Trains All Arrived" is after Claude Monet's *The Gare Saint-Lazare (or Interior View of the Gare Saint-Lazare, the Auteuil Line)*, 1877, oil on canvas. The poem also owes a debt to Danielle P. Roxbury's storied account of her life as a train conductor, *Nine Minutes to Ashby: A Woman's Life on the Line* (London: Bloodstone Books, 1955).

The epigraph to "The Future of Love" is from a sermon by the Rev. Christopher Marks, as quoted by Dr. Evie Starkweather in her essay, "Rome, Nowhere," in *Twelve Houses of the Future*, edited by T. Astabella (Toronto: Spring House Books, 2015).

"Neruda on Capri": Matilde Urrutia's memoir, *My Life with Pablo Neruda* (Stanford: Stanford University Press, 1997; translated by Alexandria Giardino) was essential to the writing of this poem, and is quoted here. The tale of Witold Shumawicz may be found in *Capri: Ex-Pats and Refugees*, a hyperbolic account of the island's Bohemian population in the 20th century by F. S. Campbell (Chicago: Boreal Books, 1999). The wedding march mentioned is from Richard Wagner's "Lohengrin" (1875). Lucila Godoy is the given name of the Chilean Nobel laureate Gabriela Mistral, who served as consul in Rapallo and Naples in 1952.

"A Fable for the Lost" is a reimagining of Zárate's famous photograph of a monk trying to talk a young girl's cat off a roof during World War II.

The epigraph to "Breakfast" is from "Try a Little Tenderness" (Campbell, Connelly, & Woods) first recorded by the Ray Noble Orchestra in 1932. The voice I hear, between the poem's title and first line, belongs to Otis Redding, who covered the song in 1966, backed by Booker T. & the M.G.'s.

"The New World" is after Isaac Bashevis Singer's children's book, *Why Noah Chose the Dove* (NY: Square Fish, 2013; pictures by Eric Carle, translated by Elizabeth Shub).

The Eleatic Stranger of Plato's *The Sophist* provides the basis for the discussion of beauty in "I Want to Believe That the More Beauty I Encounter, the Better Person I Become." The poem is dedicated to Giovanna de la Andrade, with gratitude for her keen insights into the ideas of Plato.

"Snow Day" is for Yuki and Sam Tollersen.

"Psalm" is after Yehuda Amichai's "Jewish Travel: Change Is God and Death is His Prophet," and includes lines from section thirteen of that poem. *Open Closed Open: Poems* (NY: Harcourt Books, 2000; translated by Chana Bloch and Chana Kronfeld). The poem also contains a reference to Miriam Menachem's "On Shabbat, I Move to See." *Single Days* (NY: Holden Books, 1977; translated by S. Preston Perry).

Acknowledgements

The Academy of American Poets/Poem-a-Day: "When I Am a Hummingbird."
The American Poetry Review: "Breakfast" and "The Trees of Kraków."
Barrow Street: "Old Sink in the Grass, This Morning."
Chattahoochee Review: "Neruda on Capri."
The James Dickey Review: "The Future of Love."
The Los Angeles Review: "Family Music" and "Top Hat and Tails."
Lunate: "Independent Survey."
Michigan Quarterly Review: "Ornithology."
Naugatuck Review: "The Ride."
Pinesongs: "Virtual Villanelle."
Reed: "A Partial Eclipse of the Self."
storySouth: "Psalm."
Virginia Quarterly Review: "The Birth of the Cool," "The Microeconomics
of Love," "Poem," "What Good is Life without Painting."
Zócalo Public Square: "Aubade, with Two Deer."

"Against Ekphrasis" was published as "The Light Burns Blue" in *The Eloquent Poem* (Gabriel Fried and Elise Paschen, eds.) NY: Persea Books, 2019.

"Egypt, North Carolina," "Independent Survey," and "When the Moon Was a Boy" received Honorable Mentions in the 2020 Nazim Hikmet Poetry Competition.

"In the Next Life, a Tree" was published in *Republic of Apples, Democracy of Oranges: New Eco-Poetry from China and the United States* (Tony Barnstone and Ming Di, Guest Editors; Frank Stewart, Series Editor) Manoa 31:1, 2019.

"Independent Survey" was awarded Third Place in the *Lunate 500* (UK) competition, February, 2020

"Poem" was longlisted for the 2016 National Poetry Competition (Poetry Society, U.K.).

"Psalm" received the 2019 Randall Jarrell Poetry Prize from the North Carolina Writers Network.

"The Ride" was a finalist for *The Naugatuck Review's* 8th Annual Narrative Poetry Contest.

"Two Men Disagree, and Row Out to Sea" was a finalist for the 2017 Cave Wall Broadside Competition.

"Virtual Villanelle" received the 2018 Joanna Catherine Scott Award from the North Carolina Poetry Society.

With thanks to Davidson College, the University of Tampa, and the Virginia Center for the Creative Arts. With gratitude to Bruce Cohen and Corey Marks, for their help. With fond thanks to the Tupelo gang: Jeffrey, Kristina, David, Jim, Marie, Samantha, et alia, without whom, no book.

CPSIA information can be obtained
at www.ICGtesting.com
Printed in the USA
LVHW022324130920
665913LV00009B/10